THE DRAMA OF LOVE, LIFE & DEATH IN SHAKESPEARE

THE DRAMA OF LOVE, LIFE & DEATH IN SHAKESPEARE

ANTHONY HOLDEN

MITCHELL BEAZLEY

To John Fortune

The Drama of Love, Life & Death in Shakespeare
by Anthony Holden

First published in Great Britain in 2000
by Mitchell Beazley, an imprint of
Octopus Publishing Group Limited,
2–4 Heron Quays, London E14 4JP.

ISBN 1840002832

A CIP catalogue record for this book is available from the
British Library.

Commissioning Editor: Margaret Little
Art Director: Rita Wuthrich
Executive Art Editor: Tracy Killick
Project Editor: Stephen Guise
Design: Sarah Williams
Production: Nancy Roberts
Index: Angie Hipkin

Typeset in Caslon
Printed and bound by Toppan Printing Company in China

CONTENTS

THE WORKS

This brief chronology acknowledges but eludes the contention
– authorship, date, categorization and so on – that surrounds
Shakespeare's works, while serving as a guide to the turn of his
mind. The date given for the plays, which is often approximate,
is that of composition, for the poetry that of publication.

Henry VI Part 1	1587–92	History
Henry VI Part 2	1587–92	History
Henry VI Part 3	1587–92	History
Richard III	1587–92	History
Titus Andronicus	1587–92	Tragedy
The Two Gentlemen of Verona	1587–92	Comedy
'Venus and Adonis'	1593	Poetry
The Comedy of Errors	1593–94	Comedy
The Taming of the Shrew	1593–94	Comedy
Love's Labour's Lost	1593–94	Comedy
'The Rape of Lucrece'	1594	Poetry
Romeo and Juliet	1594–95	Tragedy
A Midsummer Night's Dream	1594–95	Comedy
The Merchant of Venice	1594–95	Comedy
Richard II	1595	History
King John	1595–96	History
Henry IV Part 1	1596–97	History

The Merry Wives of Windsor	1597	Comedy
Henry IV Part 2	1598	History
Much Ado About Nothing	1598–99	Comedy
Henry V	1599	History
Julius Caesar	1599	Tragedy
As You Like It	1599	Comedy
Hamlet	1600–01	Tragedy
'The Phoenix and the Turtle'	1601	Poetry
Twelfth Night	1601–02	Comedy
Troilus and Cressida	1601–02	Comedy
All's Well That Ends Well	1602–03	Comedy
Measure for Measure	1604	Comedy
Othello	1604	Tragedy
King Lear	1605	Tragedy
Macbeth	1606	Tragedy
Antony and Cleopatra	1606–07	Tragedy
Coriolanus	1607–08	Tragedy
Timon of Athens	1607–08	Tragedy
Pericles	1608	Romance
Sonnets	1609	Poetry
Cymbeline	1609–10	Romance
The Winter's Tale	1610–11	Romance
The Tempest	1611	Romance
Henry VIII	1612–13	History
Two Noble Kinsmen	1613	Comedy

William Shakespeare of Stratford-upon-Avon, the 'rude groom' who produced the greatest body of literary work the world has ever seen, was not just a poet and playwright of genius; he was also an actor, an impresario, a canny business man and, above all, a human being. Some consider it heretical

All the world's a stage,
And all the men and women merely players…

JAQUES, AS YOU LIKE IT, ACT II, SCENE VII

to read Shakespeare's autobiography between the lines of his plays; yet we know much more of his life than is generally supposed, and it was certainly lived to the full.

There can be little doubt that the poet himself experienced most of the vast range of emotions and sensations, from the euphoric via the quotidian to the tragic, explored in the characters he created. Only part of their lives did he live by proxy. He had himself quaffed his share of flagons, run the odd gauntlet, trod a measure, heard the chimes at midnight.

In the 52 action-packed years of his life Shakespeare's personal experience ran the full gamut of youthful idealism, teenage disillusion, thwarted love, sexual jealousy, personal grief and domestic woe. Spiritually, he was raised a recusant Catholic but soon felt his faith fail, appearing to pass through a bleak, nihilistic period before settling for a world-weary brand of humanism. Love and hate; jealousy and revenge; truth and illusion; good and evil: Shakespeare's unique insight into the human psyche has left us a legacy of wisdom and humanity no other artist in history can match.

Even his arch-rival Ben Jonson had to admit that Shakespeare's works carried truths that would resonate through the centuries, transcending the inspirational times in which they happened to be written. 'Soul of the Age!' Jonson wrote. 'The applause! delight! the wonder of our stage!... He was not of an age, but for all time!'

Below **Love at first sight: Joseph Fiennes's Will Shakespeare meets Gwyneth Paltrow's Lady Viola in the Oscar-winning** *Shakespeare in Love*, **Tom Stoppard's fictional frolic about the writing of** *Romeo and Juliet*.

Yet Shakespeare never expected to be remembered as a playwright, nor indeed that his plays would outlive him. He would be amazed to find them performed, let alone revered throughout the world 400 years since he wrote them.

It was as a poet that he sought to make his name with posterity; the long narrative poems 'Venus and Adonis' and

I hold the world but as the world...
A stage where every man must play a part...

ANTONIO, THE MERCHANT OF VENICE, ACT I, SCENE I

'The Rape of Lucrece', published in the early 1590s, were the only works whose publication he approved, indeed supervised; and both were bestsellers. Like the *Sonnets*, which he never intended to be read beyond a circle of intimate friends, the 17 of his 38 plays published in his lifetime were all the work of 'pirate' publishers, exploiting the lack of copyright laws (and the defective memories of actors) to capitalize on his increasingly respected name. But it is thanks to them, and to John Heminges and Henry Condell, the two fellow-actors who gathered them all together in the First Folio – published in 1623, seven years after his death – that Shakespeare's plays do survive to entrance and enlighten, entertain and harrow us. Without them, our world would be an infinitely poorer place.

The Chorus introducing Romeo and Juliet may speak blithely of the 'two hours' traffic of our stage', but most of Shakespeare's stage works last almost twice that long, even when brutally cut. A full-length Hamlet plays even longer. Only in our own lifetimes has the uniquely 20th-century art of the cinema managed, for commercial reasons, to squeeze Shakespeare into its own two-hour box of tricks – often with more success than purists might care to admit, or audiences dare to hope.

This book is as much a celebration of movie versions of Shakespeare's plays as of those themes that capture his timeless pleasures and passions. For the cinema has done as much as the stage in our own times to keep the Swan of Avon alive, to reinvent him for succeeding generations as imaginatively as the great players and actor-managers who went before the great, cigar-toting producers. At the turn of a new century, as Shakespeare is universally voted Man of the Millennium, the remarkable success of *Shakespeare in Love* has introduced yet another generation to the joys, agonies and universal truths of his work, at a time when Shakespeare teaching in schools seemed more than ever in danger of putting young people off him for life.

The production company behind *Shakespeare in Love* ran through a number of alternative titles for the film before finally succumbing to the arguments of its

screenwriters, Tom Stoppard and Marc Norman, and their
director, John Madden. Anything with Shakespeare in or
near the title has always, to Hollywood, been 'box-office
poison'. Yet some memorable movies have been made from
Shakespeare plays, winning the Stratford screenwriter and
his celluloid interpreters their share of Academy Awards.
No fewer than six of Shakespeare's plays, from the never-
before-filmed *Titus Andronicus* to the equally unlikely
Love's Labour's Lost, alongside gritty new interpretations of

Hamlet and *Macbeth*, greeted the dawn of the 21st century. In Hollywood as elsewhere, Shakespeare is bigger business than ever in the four centuries since his death.

So it seems appropriate to bring mere words to life with images he would surely have approved – stills from productions reaching a wider audience than the Globe's management could ever have dreamed of, featuring stars better-known for lesser work than their homage to the playwright whom all actors owe the deepest of debts.

> *How many ages hence*
> *Shall this our lofty scene be acted over*
> *In states unborn and accents yet unknown!*
>
> CASSIUS, JULIUS CAESAR, ACT III, SCENE I

'Look here on this picture,' Hamlet tells his distraught mother, 'and on this…' The words of Shakespeare's most celebrated character serve as an apt motto for these pages. But remember also those of his friend and rival Ben Jonson, printed alongside the portrait of the poet in the front of the first published folio of his collected works: 'Reader, look / Not on his Picture, but his Book…'

There is no real need, anyway, for portraits. To see Shakespeare's face, in the words of his eloquent admirer Anthony Burgess, 'we need only look in a mirror'.

'the course of true love never did run smooth,' Lysander tells Hermia at the outset of *A Midsummer Night's Dream*. Shakespeare was writing from the heart. The poet's own love life had been in a state of some turmoil since the age of 18, when he made 26-year-old Anne Hathaway pregnant and was strong-armed into marrying her. *hamlet* The homely daughter of a landowner in the nearby village of Shottery, Anne was 'on the shelf' by Elizabethan standards – the same age, after all, as Juliet's mother, who is already impatient to become a granny.

Did Anne trap the teenage William – quite a catch, as the son of a recent Mayor of Stratford – into doing the honourable thing by her? We can hear him suggesting as much 20 years later in *Twelfth Night*. 'Let still the woman take an elder than herself', Orsino, Duke of Illyria, advises Cesario (not knowing he is really the woman, disguised as a boy, whom he will himself marry).

Because Shakespeare famously left Anne his second-best bed in his will, history has assumed that their marriage was unhappy; in truth, the best bed would have been reserved for guests, and bequeathed to the eldest daughter, so he was more likely going out *cymbeline* of his way to make the touching gesture of leaving his wife the marital bed they had shared, on and off, for more than 30 years. Anne, after all, had raised their three children and cared for his ageing parents all those years he had been working and playing hard in London.

By the time he wrote *A Midsummer Nights Dream*, within a few years of leaving Anne behind in Stratford, Shakespeare already seems to have been in love with a lady of the London night – the famous 'Dark Lady' of the Sonnets, whose identity has tantalized scholars for four centuries. In Elizabethan England the word 'dark' denoted class or social status as much as skin colour or complexion; so candidates have ranged from high-born royal ladies-in-waiting via the exotic, Italian wives of court scholars and musicians to prostitutes and madams from the 'stews' (or brothels) of Clerkenwell.

But this same 'Dark Lady', whoever she was, also became the poet's 'female evil', who 'tempteth my better angel from my side, / And would corrupt my saint to be a devil.' She was unfaithful to him, causing him paroxysms of jealousy. And with so much danger of catching the 'clap' (gonorrhoea) or even the dreaded 'pox' (syphilis, often fatal), sex *othello* sometimes became to Shakespeare 'the expense of spirit in a waste of shame'. Love, in other words, could all too often breed hatred – or, as Freud might have it, love-hate. Shakespeare seems to have had his own bouts of the clap, and to have himself known love inexorably curdle to hatred. The playwright who wrote some of the strongest, most complex parts ever devised for women – even before the law allowed women onstage to play them – also filled his later plays with scathing references to the fairer sex, and the multitude of woes they can inflict upon mere men.

'Get thee to a nunnery' yells Hamlet at Ophelia, with whom he seems to have a classically Freudian love-hate relationship. 'I say we will have no more marriages.' Polonius' poor daughter is understandably confused; one minute Hamlet is writing her love poems, the next he is telling her he has never loved her. Is he mad – or just playing mad? 'I am but mad north-north-west,' he tells Rosencrantz and Guildenstern. 'When the wind is southerly, I know a hawk from a handsaw.'

Above 'Get thee to a nunnery' (Hamlet, *Hamlet*, act III, scene i). Laurence Olivier as Hamlet, Jean Simmons as Ophelia (1948).

Lovers and madmen have such seething brains...

THESEUS, A MIDSUMMER NIGHT'S DREAM, ACT V, SCENE I

Far right, top
Mel Gibson as Hamlet, Helena Bonham Carter as Ophelia in Franco Zeffirelli's 1990 version.

Far right, bottom
Anthony Hopkins as Claudius and Judy Parfitt as Gertrude in Tony Richardson's 1969 *Hamlet*, starring Nicol Williamson as the prince.

In truth, of course, Hamlet's mood-swings are down to his revulsion about his mother's guiltily 'o'erhasty' marriage to his late father's brother, Claudius, the new king who is also (it soon transpires) old Hamlet's murderer. When the ghost of his father returns to tell him this – 'Oh my prophetic soul! My uncle?' – the course of Hamlet's fate is determined with an oath of vengeance. Those moving scenes between Hamlet *père et fils* denote, of course, another potent kind of love explored in the play: the love between parent and child. Shakespeare's own father lay dying as he wrote the work whose name was interchangeable with that of his lost, lamented son, Hamnet, who had died five years earlier at the age of 11.

To counterpoint the love between Hamlet and his girlfriend, his mother, his father, Shakespeare puts his mother's love for his fratricidal uncle flagrantly on display, thus arousing Hamlet's emotions yet further. His own natural love for his mother turns to violent hatred in the central 'closet' scene, where only the timely intervention of his father's ghost prevents him doing her more damage than breaking her heart 'in twain'.

Hamlet is as full of love and hate as any other Shakespeare play. Alongside the complexities of Hamlet's love for his mother, and hers for her late husband's brother, the playwright artfully intertwines the love of Laertes for his sister, Ophelia, and their father Polonius' bumbling concern for them both. Hamlet's love for Ophelia is, he says, worth more than that of 'forty thousand brothers', but it is his careless murder of her father – believing him to be Claudius eavesdropping on his dealings with Gertrude – that drives Ophelia insane, and eventually to suicide.

Can love have consequences much bleaker than that? It does in *Othello*, where the noble Moor's love for his bride is exquisitely expressed before it turns so sour. 'Perdition catch my soul, but I do love thee,' says Othello to himself as he watches Desdemonda across the room – a sentiment almost as beautiful as Posthumus' tribute to his wife Imogen in *Cymbeline*: 'Hang there like fruit, my soul, until the tree die.'

Previous page **Gertrude (Glenn Close) all too easily transfers her affections from Hamlet's father to his brother (and murderer) Claudius (Alan Bates).**

Far left **'I say we will have no more marriages' (Hamlet, *Hamlet*, act III, scene i). Nicol Williamson's 1969 Hamlet dispatches Marianne Faithfull's Ophelia to her nunnery.**

The poet Tennyson loved this line so much that he whispered it to his own wife on his deathbed. But Posthumus and Imogen have had to endure appalling trials to be reunited in domestic bliss – a consummation devoutly to be wished, but never to be granted Othello and Desdemona, who seem, amid the play's notorious contractions of time, never even to enjoy an uninterrupted wedding night.

> *Is love a tender thing? It is too rough,*
> *Too rude, too boisterous, and it pricks like*
> *a thorn.*

ROMEO, ROMEO AND JULIET, ACT I, SCENE IV

The only happily married couple in all Shakespeare, it would appear, are the Macbeths. Though doomed by their own 'o'erleaping ambition', they certainly enjoy a marriage uniquely strong in the canon before conspiring to murder Duncan and trigger their own inevitable doom – involving them, too, in estrangement and madness. 'She should have died hereafter,' is all Macbeth has to say on hearing of his wife's demise, before musing fatalistically:

Tomorrow and tomorrow and tomorrow

Creeps in this petty pace from day to day...

In one recent London production, the new Thane of Cawdor even had sex onstage with his wife while preparing to greet

Duncan's momentous entrance beneath their battlements. It did not seem out of place. They are, after all, young and vigorous; after a prolonged separation, they had exciting news to celebrate; and, with murder in the air, power and danger can be as heady a sexual cocktail as any.

Poor Romeo and Juliet, of course, do nothing wrong to earn the dire fate that befalls them both by the end of their own sad saga. An undelivered letter is the only, rather limp, plot device that consigns these 'star-crossed lovers' to their poignantly early graves. The play, too, is an early one, the first in which Shakespeare spreads his poetic wings with complete,

Above Claire Danes' angelic Juliet sprouts wings opposite Leonardo DiCaprio's Romeo in Baz Lurhmann's 1996 *Romeo + Juliet.*

relaxed freedom; by depriving the lovers of the responsibility for their own fates, however, he fails as yet to write a tragedy of the truly Shakespearean proportions to follow. This play, the first romantic tragedy ever to be written for the stage, is more Mills and Boon than *Grand Guignol*; but again love comes up against hatred in the shape of the Montague-Capulet feud that seals the lovers' doom. Shakespeare himself had personal experience of such feuds, in the aristocratic circle of his friend and patron the Earl of Southampton, and indeed among his own colleagues and rivals in the London playwriting fraternity.

My only love sprung from my only hate!

JULIET, ROMEO AND JULIET, ACT I, SCENE V

When he purloined and remodelled a theme familiar to his audiences, as always, he transformed it into a morality play with ringing contemporary resonances, then as now.

Feuding lovers brought out of him more muscular (if less lyrical) writing than these sometimes simpering teenagers. Katharina and Petruchio in *The Taming of the Shrew* are rough-edged forerunners of Beatrice and Benedick in *Much Ado About Nothing*: brave, independent spirits just made for each other, if only they would swallow their pride long enough to acknowledge it. The subtext of *The Shrew* is much less crude than latter-day feminists would have us believe. Petruchio may

Far right 'Parting is such sweet sorrow' (Juliet, *Romeo and Juliet*, act II, scene ii) as Lesley Howard's 1936 Romeo woos Norma Shearer's Juliet.

be out to snag a wealthy bride, but he can sense a kindred spirit in the wild, untamed Katharina. By teaching her some manners, in his own rough-hewn way, he also brings out the essential strength in her character, as is shown by the touching scene at the end in which she is the only wife prepared to show public obedience to her husband. There is a great nobility of character, no mere servitude, in this moment, just as there is in Benedick's vow to avenge the apparent wrong done Beatrice's cousin by murdering his own best friend. Petruchio would have paid similar public homage to Katharina – that is the point – just as Beatrice, too, eventually submits herself publicly to Benedick's will. These plays are about the essential respect built into true love, as much as the fires through which any love must pass to build such graceful strength.

Shakespeare's plays celebrate love in all its guises: Machiavellian, as in many of the history plays, starting with Richard III's unlikely wooing of the Lady Anne; anarchic, as in the early comedies *The Two Gentlemen of Verona* and *The Comedy of Errors*; courtly and sophisticated, as in *Love's Labour's Lost* and *All's Well That Ends Well*; young and innocent, as in *Romeo and Juliet* and *The Tempest*; poignantly doomed, as in *Troilus and Cressida* and *Antony and Cleopatra*; ugly and unscrupulous, as in *Measure for Measure* and *Cymbeline*; the great redeemer, as in the late plays from *Pericles* to *The Winter's Tale*.

Above **Richard Burton's Petruchio has his hands full with Elizabeth Taylor's wild, untamed Katharina in Franco Zeffirelli's 1966** *The Taming of the Shrew.*

Far left '**I shall say good night till it be tomorrow' (Juliet,** *Romeo and Juliet,* **act II, scene ii). Olivia Hussey and Leonard Whiting in Zeffirelli's 1968** *Romeo and Juliet.*

Above Burton's Petruchio
finally gets Taylor's
Katharina to the altar.

The Merchant of Venice is not really about Shylock;
Shakespeare is primarily exploring three parallel love stories –
four if you include the homosexual love of Antonio, the
eponymous merchant, for Bassanio, whose quest for the
wealthy, beautiful Portia leads him to drive his near-fatal
bargain with the Jew.

All these loves build on hatred, or grow stronger through
adversity. Antony causes Cleopatra grief by making a
strategic marriage with Octavia; yet, for all her fury, they
wind up dying for each other. Cordelia's love for her father,
King Lear, is too natural and self-evident to be measured
in mere words, like her sisters'; when required to spell it out,
the youngest (and most honest) daughter's heart sticks in

Far right
Douglas Fairbanks
tamed Mary Pickford in
a popular 1929 version
of *The Shrew.*

Left Laurence Fishburne's 1995 Othello has yet to be poisoned against Irene Jacob's Desdemona

her mouth, again precipitating both their eventual dooms. Lear's apparent hatred of his daughter is merely an aspect of his madness; as her false sisters betray him, it is his love of Cordelia that finally, if too late, brings him back to his senses.

Disguises; 'bed-tricks'; mistaken identities; false reports of infidelity: many of the devices used by Shakespeare were traditional themes into which he breathed new life, so forcefully that they still have much to teach us today. There is much more to true love, he is telling us, than Jaques in *As You Like It*'s stereotypical lover 'Sighing like furnace, with a woeful ballad / Made to his mistress' eyebrow.' Between love and hatred, seemingly complementary passions, there is a thin dividing line that all lovers must gingerly tread. Only a few, a happy few, will make it across to the other side.

Far left 'Put out the light' (Othello, *Othello*, act V, scene ii). Laurence Olivier's 1965 Othello mourns his murder of Maggie Smith's Desdemona.

DEATH AND RETRIBUTION

'You! – What do you know about death?' a rattled Guildenstern asks the Player King in Tom Stoppard's ingenious play *Rosencrantz and Guildenstern Are Dead*. 'It's what the actors do best,' replies the Player. 'They can die heroically, comically, ironically, slowly, suddenly, disgustingly, charmingly, or from a great height.'

Imagine him one of Shakespeare's fellow-actors at the Globe Theatre, and this worldly-wise old actor's delight in dying stylishly might have derived solely from the work of *hamlet* his own in-house playwright. Only in his comedies and romances does Shakespeare choose to spare most of his characters; in his tragedies, histories and Roman plays there is generally a profusion of death and retribution – as in *Hamlet*, the closing scene of which leaves the stage littered with enough corpses to dismay even the stolid Fortinbras. 'Is that all they can do – die?' Stoppard's Rosencrantz asks the Player. 'No, no,' he protests, 'they kill beautifully. In fact some of them kill even better than they die.'

If most Shakespearean deaths are violent and unnatural – the result of war, ambition, politics, feuding, hot-headedness, jealousy, revenge – he seems to reserve the few natural deaths in the canon for characters he was fond of, like Falstaff. The one true tragedy of the playwright's own life was the death in 1596 of his only son Hamnet, at the age of just 11. We do not know how the poor boy died, but we can sense the effect on his father from the mourning strains that suddenly haunt his work-in-progress, *King John*. 'Grief fills the room up of my absent child,' laments Constance, believing her own young son Arthur to have died,

> Lies in his bed, walks up and down with me,
>
> Puts on his pretty looks, repeats his words,
>
> Remembers me of all his gracious parts,
>
> Stuffs out his vacant garments with his form...

This heart-rending speech is surely Shakespeare himself mourning his only son, as he would throughout the rest of his work. Beyond the personal grief that now becomes a recurring strain in his plays, Shakespeare had been robbed of a direct line of descent just as his worldly success saw him acquire a coat of arms and thus the status of gentleman. Left with Hamnet's two sisters, Susanna and Judith, his work would soon become obsessed with daughters – Cordelia in *King Lear*, Marina in *Pericles*, Imogen in *Cymbeline*, Perdita in *The Winter's Tale*, Miranda in *The Tempest* – while the only two significant sons after Hamlet (apart from Edmund and Edgar in *King Lear*), Coriolanus' precocious offspring and poor Mamillius in *The Winter's Tale* (who also dies in childhood), are much Hamnet's age, as if the poet could see male offspring only in some time-warp frozen when his own son vanished to 'the undiscovered country, from whose bourn / No traveller returns'.

Above 'Then venom to thy work' (Hamlet, *Hamlet*, act V, scene ii). Olivier's 1948 Hamlet leaps dramatically to his revenge on Basil Sydney's Claudius.

Death, to Shakespeare, was better kept on the stage, where it could remain in his masterly control. As he muses in *King John*, anticipating *Macbeth* and other tales of carnage to come,

There is no sure foundation set on blood,

No certain life achiev'd by others' death.

Ten years later, Macbeth himself picks up the theme: 'It will have blood, they say. Blood will have blood.' As in Greek tragedy, which he had been well taught at school, each death in Shakespeare seems to trigger another, pointing up the unscrupulous cruelty of worldly ambition amid the frailty of human life.

Death can be a merciful release from the vanity of human wishes, as in the exquisite song in *Cymbeline*:

Fear no more the heat of the sun

Nor the furious winter's rages,

Thou thy worldly task has done,

Home art gone and ta'en thy wages…

Right and far right 'Alas, poor Yorick' (Hamlet, *Hamlet*, act V, scene i) muse (far right) Laurence Olivier's 1948 Hamlet and (right) Kenneth Branagh's 1996 Prince of Denmark.

Death is the great leveller, as in Hamlet's meditation on the skull of Yorick, the court jester, whom he had known well as a child: 'I knew him, Horatio, a fellow of infinite jest, of most excellent fancy... Here hung those lips that I have kissed I know not how oft. Where be your gibes now, your gambols, your songs, your flashes of merriment that were wont to set the table on a roar?' Come thus to dust, he muses, even Alexander the Great might wind up 'stopping a bunghole' in a beer-barrel.

In Hamlet's affectionate memories of Yorick – 'he hath bore me on his back a thousand times' – Shakespeare was paying posthumous tribute to Dick Tarleton, resident comedian of the Queen's Men when the poet first arrived in London, who may even have known him as a child when the company visited Stratford. Yet comedy had to wait when the apprentice actor started writing. Death, it seems, was better at

the box-office, for he scored a big public success with his first works: a huge, ambitious, unprecedented tetralogy of history plays – the *Henry VI* cycle and *Richard III* – in which, of course, death and retribution played central roles, as they would when he continued the saga a decade later.

In the thick of the Wars of the Roses, on the threshold of his own demise, the weak King Henry VI sees a son unwittingly kill his father, and a father kill his son. If death was to symbolize the futility of war, the young Shakespeare was

He that dies pays all debts.

STEPHANO, THE TEMPEST, ACT III, SCENE II

going to lay it on with a trowel. As in Greek tragedy, again, Henry is paying the price – as indeed are his subjects – for the original sin of his ancestor Henry Bolingbroke, alias Henry IV, in deposing and murdering Richard II in 1399. In time, soon after Hamnet's death, he would return to the theme, writing 'prequels' to *Richard II*, the *Henry VI* trilogy and *Richard III* in the two parts of *Henry IV* and the brash, jingoistic *Henry V*. To Shakespeare's audience a monarch was divinely chosen and ruled with divine authority – 'there's a divinity doth hedge a king' – so there could be no crime more heinous than usurping or killing a king. Even on the eve of Agincourt, Shakespeare has the blameless warrior-king Henry V acknowledge the

retribution inevitably awaiting his father's offence against the natural order 16 years earlier:

Not today, O Lord!

O not today, think not upon the fault

My father made in compassing the crown!

Henry's prayers would be answered, and the price of his father's sins not extracted at Agincourt, nor indeed during the

A man can die but once. We owe God a death…

FEEBLE, KING HENRY IV PART 2, ACT III, SCENE II

seven further years of his reign. But the closing Chorus bluntly reminds us that Henry died young, and his son's protector

lost France and made his England bleed,

Which oft our stage hath shown.

Not until the murderous Richard III's well-deserved death at Bosworth would Henry's crime finally be expiated, and the natural order restored.

With the completion of this mighty history cycle – eight plays covering five reigns from 1377 to 1485 – Shakespeare sought to demonstrate the consequences of interfering with the divine order not merely as they affected the principal players, but also the hapless subjects whose lives are disrupted, often ended by decades of disorder and civil strife. Never more than in the two parts of *Henry IV* did he so vividly depict the

Far left 'Despair thy charm' (Macduff, *Macbeth*, act V, scene viii). Macduff (Terence Bayler) takes his revenge on Macbeth (Jon Finch) in Roman Polanski's vivid 1971 movie.

suffering of the common man as the pawn of warring power-brokers. If Henry himself can never, like Macbeth, live to enjoy the throne he played so foully for – 'Uneasy lies the head that wears a crown' – so his offence affects the rest of the nation, which pays an equally heavy price.

Retribution for regicide comes also, inexorably, to Macbeth and Claudius, inflicted on the latter by his victim's son, the young Hamlet, who might himself have been king had not his father's murderer 'popped in between the election and my hopes' while he was away at university. Given the political uncertainties of his own day, however, with the

Vengeance is in my heart, death in my hand,
Blood and revenge are hammering in my head.

AARON, TITUS ANDRONICUS, ACT II, SCENE III

long-lived Queen Elizabeth's refusal to name an heir moving even favourites like the ambitious Earl of Essex to rebellion, Shakespeare felt minded to muse on the *just* murder of tyrants; it was a live debating-point among Catholic 'heretics' as the Queen sought to crush recusants and find a successor who would defend the Protestant religion founded by her father, Henry VIII. Shakespeare's own father was a recusant Catholic; the poet himself had been brought up in the 'old' faith. So Brutus is 'the noblest Roman of them all' in

persuading his fellow conspirators that Julius Caesar must die,
for even considering the crown offered him by Senators and
people alike. For a man to adopt semi-divine status, in Brutus'
scheme of things, was a crime even worse than murder:

> It must be by his death; and for my part
>
> I know no personal cause to spurn at him
>
> But for the general.

Cassius' motives are more envious, but even he

> had as lief not be as live to be
>
> In awe of such a thing as I myself.

In Shakespeare's scheme of things, of course, they too must
eventually die, however worthy the motives for their crime
against the natural order. Brutus does so in the most noble
way available – on his own sword.

Below **In Zefferelli's
1986 film of Verdi's
opera** *Otello*, **Placido
Domingo laments his
murder of Katia
Ricciarelli's Desdemona.**

As does Marc Antony, the friend of Caesar who so eloquently defends his memory and so doggedly pursues his murderers to Philippi, only to return some eight years later in his own personal tragedy. The ghost of Julius Caesar still stalks the stage in *Antony and Cleopatra*, as the previous lover of Egypt's exotic queen and father of her son, before Antony in turn falls for her considerable charms. Thousands have died in Rome's wars, just as in England's civil wars, as Shakespeare is careful to remind us before concentrating all his resources, at the height of his powers, on the momentous, solitary, self-inflicted deaths of these two titans, who threw away the entire world for their love. It is this sense of avoidability that makes their deaths all the more momentous, and thus the power of their love so affecting.

The word 'retribution' does not appear anywhere in Shakespeare's work, but the concept is pervasive. Murderers must pay for their crimes with their own deaths, however long

Right 'Et tu, Brute?'
(Caesar, *Julius Caesar*,
act III, scene i). James
Mason's Brutus inflicts
the mortal wound on
John Gielgud's Julius
Caesar (1970).

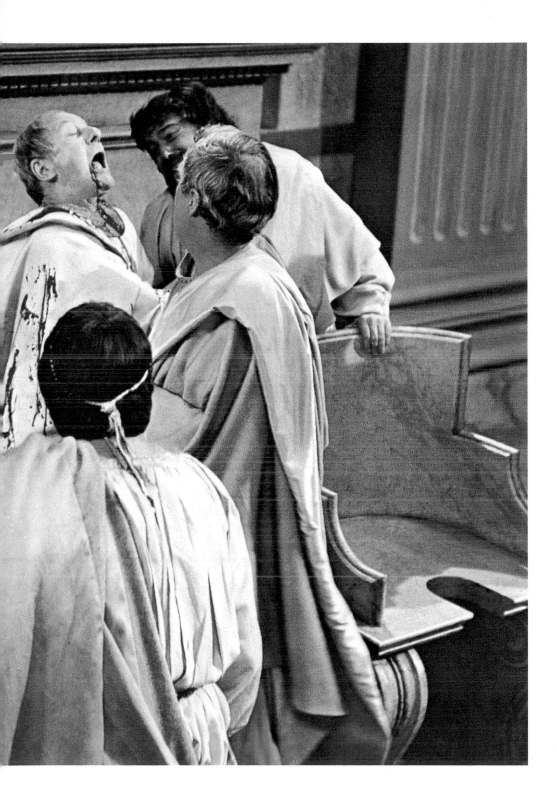

it takes – another natural law that he absorbed from the ancient Greek tragedians. His greatness often lies in his exploration of the motives for these crimes, and the agonies of conscience endured by their perpetrators. But his profound humanity is most evident in his sympathy for the countless bystanders caught up in the bloody ambitions of others. In so much of Shakespeare, death is merely a casual by-product of human ambition, malevolence or mere misguidedness. The roll-call of innocent victims stretches to the crack of doom: from Clarence, drowned by his brother in a butt of malmsey wine, via Romeo and Juliet, Duncan, Banquo, Lady Macduff and her children, to

Below 'Howl! howl! howl!' (Lear, *King Lear*, act V, scene iii). Lear has only himself to blame for the death of his beloved daughter Cordelia in Grigori Kozyntsev's 1969 version.

Desdemona, Cordelia and Hermione (whose apparent return to life still remains a form of death). Lear's folly – not so much in dividing his kingdom as expecting still to rule it – sees many a noble spirit brought low: Kent, Gloucester and his son Edgar all suffer appallingly for their selfless attempts to protect their divinely-anointed master from his own mistakes.

'I owe God a death,' said Essex at his trial for treason in 1601, which duly saw him executed. He was quoting Shakespeare. 'Why thou owest God a death,' says Hal to Falstaff in *Henry IV* Part 1, to which the rascally old knight replies with his great catechism: ''Tis not due yet. I would be loath to pay him before his day...' The finest hour of Feeble, the 'woman's tailor' recruited by Falstaff in *Henry IV* Part 2, likewise comes with the words: 'A man can die but once. We owe God a death... He that dies this year is quit for the next.'

Essex, too, faced death nobly; Shakespeare may well have been thinking of him in *Macbeth* when he has Malcolm report of the Thane of Cawdor:

> Nothing in his life
>
> Became him like the leaving it. He died
>
> As one that had been studied in his death
>
> To throw away the dearest thing he owed
>
> As 'twere a careless trifle.

Death may be the great leveller; but, in Shakespeare, it can bring out the best in people.

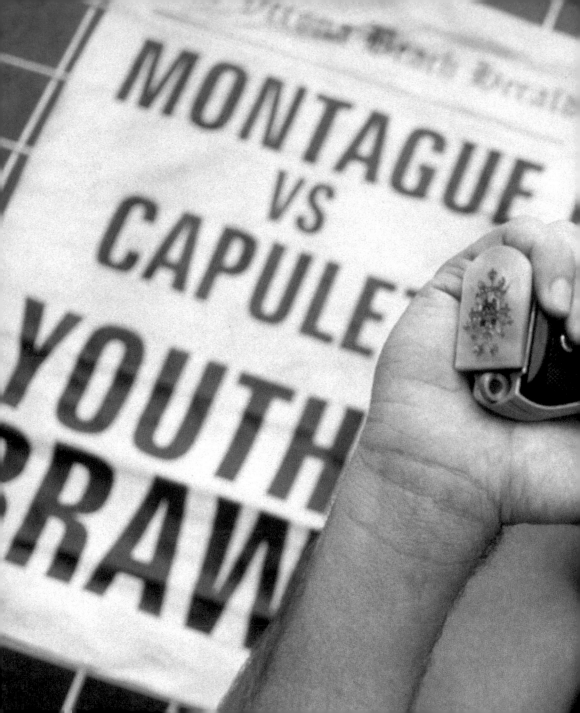

With Shakespeare spending so much time in London – he went home, according to the diarist John Aubrey, about once a year – it has been saucily suggested that his indigent brother Richard exploited his absence to take advantage of his wife. But that would seem quite out of character for the seemingly prim, rather dour Anne Hathaway, conscientious mother to Shakespeare's three children and dutiful daughter-in-law to his ageing parents. Back in London, meanwhile, it is much *othello* easier to believe that Shakespeare himself took advantage of his friend Richard Field's wife, when the prospering printer returned home to see his family in Stratford.

But Shakespeare certainly had first-hand experience of the horrors of sexual jealousy. We can believe nothing less of the playwright who came up with *Othello* and *The Winter's Tale*, of the poet who wrote of 'the green-eyed monster' and 'the beast with two backs', who chose to deploy such violent language and imagery to describe so drastic a breech in the domestic order. In *The Winter's Tale* Leontes talks of his wife and best friend 'paddling palms and pinching fingers', then looks directly at the audience – knowing there are cuckolds within his eye-line – to muse that 'Many a man there is (even at this present, / Now, while I speak this) holds his wife by th'arm, / That little thinks she had been sluic'd in his absence / And his pond fish'd by his next neighbour, by / Sir Smile, his neighbour.' The image of next-door Sir Smile sweet-talking his cuckold-neighbour after possessing his wife is almost as brutal as his choice of that all too graphic word 'sluic'd'.

As for revenge – a very different word from retribution – 'sweet, gentle' Will Shakespeare made few enemies in his lifetime and had little cause to extract personal satisfaction from anyone beyond unscrupulous printers who pirated his works. It was anyway more his style to take a literary revenge, as he did on the embittered poet-playwright Robert Greene, whose dying denunciation of Shakespeare in 1592 constitutes the first surviving reference to the Stratford man's *hamlet* presence in London as a playwright. This ill-educated young parvenu, wrote Greene, was 'an upstart crow, beautified with our feathers' – a plagiarist, in other words, who stole his and other men's lines.

Shakespeare lodged no surviving complaint; but he had his revenge within months of Greene's death in the shape of a grovelling apology from the printer, Robert Chettle. Yet the phrase must have lingered in his mind, perhaps in the bitchy backchat of London's theatreland taverns, as he clearly savours the in-joke, almost a decade later, of having Polonius read to the King and Queen Hamlet's love letter to his daughter, 'the celestial and my soul's idol, the most beautified' Ophelia. 'That's an ill phrase, a vile phrase,' Polonius breaks off to protest. '"Beautified" is a vile phrase.'

It was the 'Dark Lady' of the Sonnets, if no one else, who first put Shakespeare through the rigours of sexual jealousy. To waste time trying to identify her is to overlook the tortured beauty of the poetry she provoked. It is surely best to leave her, as Anthony Burgess advises, 'anonymous, even composite', an immortal icon of 'some of the commonest experiences known to men – obsession with a woman's body, revulsion, pain in

desertion, resignation at another's treachery,' not to mention 'the irresistible lure of the primal darkness that resides in all women, whether white or black'.

Better, even, to think of the Dark Lady in Shakespeare's own fictional terms – as that prototype of Shakespeare's many strong-minded, self-confident women, Rosaline in *Love's Labour's Lost*, the 'whitely wanton with a velvet brow', with

Left 'Look here on this picture, and on this!' (Hamlet, *Hamlet*, act III, scene iv). Mel Gibson's Hamlet cleaves Glenn Close's heart in twain.

dark 'pitchballs' for eyes, who has much the same plans for
Berowne as the Dark Lady had for the poet of the Sonnets:

> How I would make him fawn, and beg, and seek
>
> And wait the season, and observe the times,
>
> And spend his prodigal wit in bootless rimes...

Whoever she was, the Dark Lady was probably responsible
for Shakespeare's creation of Desdemona, the hapless innocent

Left Kenneth Branagh's
Hamlet and Michael
Malone's Laertes embark
on the duel that will kill
them both.

who falls in love with the noble Moor's tales of his military
exploits. According to a contemporary account of the Moors,
which Shakespeare must have read – John Leo's A *Geographical
History of Africa*, published in 1600 – 'No nation in the world
is so subject unto jealousy, for they will rather lose their lives
than put up any disgrace in the behalf of their women.'
Himself a Barbary-bred Moor, Leo added of his 'very proud

Previous page 'A hit, a very palpable hit' (Osric, *Hamlet*, act V, scene ii). Olivier's Oscar-winning 1948 *Hamlet* duels with Terence Morgan's Laertes.

and high-minded, and wonderfully addicted unto wrath' fellow-countrymen: 'Their wits are but mean, and they are so credulous that they will believe matters impossible which are told them.'

Shakespeare seems to have leapt upon this description when minded, at the time of a Moorish embassy to racist Elizabethan London, to write literature's first account of a

How all occasions do inform against me,
And spur my dull revenge!

HAMLET, HAMLET, ACT IV, SCENE IV

black man with great nobility, brought low by the treachery of his white inferiors. Racism is a powerful subtext of Othello, all too often overlooked amid the power of the poet's depiction of sexual jealousy. Why does Iago seek to persuade his commanding officer that his chaste, virtuous new bride has been unfaithful to him? The motives the envoy himself advances – that he has been passed over for Cassio's lieutenancy, that he suspects the Moor has done 'my office betwixt my sheets' – are so inadequate as to amount to a form of baffled self-justification; beyond his innate racism, Iago cannot explain even to himself why he chooses to cause such unspeakably cruel havoc. Iago was never officer material, anyway – and it is no more than perversely wishful thinking on

Left 'Drink off this
potion!' (Hamlet,
Hamlet, act V, scene ii).
Richard Burton's
Hamlet administers the
coup de grace to Alfred
Drake's Claudius.

his part that Othello might have bedded his own wife Emilia.
Verdi's superb librettist for his operatic version, the composer
Arrigo Boito, inserted the famous 'Credo' aria in response to
this problem: 'I believe in an evil god' it begins. It is wonderful
music, but does nothing to improve a play to whose text the
opera otherwise adheres very faithfully. No one has ever bettered
the poet Coleridge's verdict on Iago: 'the motive-hunting of
motiveless malignity'.

The horrors of watching Othello swallowing Iago's bait are
so powerful that this can be one of the most painful to watch
of all Shakespeare's plays. It provokes audience involvement

Far right, top

Leonard Whiting's
Romeo fatefully kills
Tybalt in revenge for
his friend Mercutio

more intense than any other. The ending of *Lear* may amount almost to sadism on the playwright's part, when he kills off Cordelia, even the Fool (whom we have not seen since the interval), for no great reason beyond nihilistic world-weariness. But the masochism involved in watching *Othello*, admiring Iago's breathtaking ingenuity while lamenting the Moor's credulity, is of a different order. It is not even that Desdemona particularly captures our sympathy; she is somewhat one-dimensional by the standards of Shakespeare's often complex

> *Jealous souls will not be answered so;*
> *They are not ever jealous for the cause*
> *But jealous for they are jealous.*

EMILIA, OTHELLO, ACT III, SCENE IV

women. Her 'Willow Song' as she prepares to die is relatively unaffecting – the poet at his most formulaic. The audience is entirely caught up in the enormity of what Iago has done to his hapless master. When one of the great 19th-century Othellos, William Macready, took Iago by the throat, a gentlemen in the audience could bear it all no longer, and famously cried out: 'Choke the devil! Choke him!'

Far right, bottom

Leonardo DiCaprio's
Romeo avenges the
murder of Mercutio.

Jealousy and envy (as in the case of Robert Greene): to Elizabethan audiences, Othello and Iago were complementary characters, opposite sides of the same coin. If there was much of

Above Iago (Kenneth Branagh) plots the doom of his master Othello (Laurence Fishburne) and his bride Desdemona (Irene Jacob).

Shakespeare himself in such of his characters as Hamlet and Lear, he seems to be aware of two sides to his own personality in *Othello*'s complementary central figures. As indeed did Ben Jonson, while apparently paying Shakespeare a posthumous compliment. Says 'honest' Iago of Othello:

The Moor is of a free and open nature

That thinks men honest that but seem to be so.

Says Jonson of Shakespeare: 'He was indeed honest, and of an open mind and free nature.'

Sexual jealousy is perhaps at its most potent, and thus its most devastating to behold as well as to suffer, when the victim is wracked by lack of proof of the infidelity – or even, as in both Shakespeare's great plays about jealousy, when the charge is untrue. Hermione in *The Winter's Tale* is as innocent as Desdemona of the suspicions against her that are taking such ugly shape in her husband's mind. Leontes has no Iago to trick him with innuendo and lost handkerchiefs; his wits seem suddenly to desert him as he beholds his wife doing exactly what he has asked her to do: persuade his old friend Polixenes to prolong his stay at their court. Once the fever takes hold, all logic evaporates. No one can persuade him that his suspicions about Hermione could not be more misjudged.

Above Orson Welles' 1951 Othello laments his murder of his innocent wife Desdemona.

Othello, of course, winds up strangling his wife and making his own quietus. The downfall of so noble a man, a great military leader if not a naturally domestic creature, is as painful to behold as anything in all Shakespeare. By the late plays and *The Winter's Tale* – some seven, perhaps ten years later – the ageing playwright had entered a calmer, more reflective period, where he offers his characters a redemption he denied Hamlet, Othello, Lear, Macbeth, all of whom die inevitable deaths. Leontes is deranged enough to reject Apollo's oracle, proclaiming his wife's innocence; it is fit punishment for him that she is reported dead because of the suffering he has inflicted on her. He has no reason to disbelieve the news, and enters a prolonged period of anguished penitence. Their son dies, too, and apparently their daughter. The first three acts of

Left Laurence Harvey's
Leontes wrongly
suspects the fidelity
of his wife, Hermione,
in the only film
adaptation (1966) of
The Winter's Tale.

The Winter's Tale amount to a conventional Shakespearean tragedy, with the bleakest of endings. But there are still two acts to go, and late Shakespeare developed a fascinated penchant for the supernatural. Hermione is presented to her husband as a statue, which miraculously comes to life. She is restored to him, as is their daughter. But there is no guarantee of future happiness. The shrewdest stage directors leave the couple too broken to foresee much of a future. Leontes' sin may have been pardoned, but it can never be expiated.

O beware, my lord, of jealousy:
It is the green-eyed monster, which doth mock
The meat it feeds on.

IAGO, OTHELLO, ACT III, SCENE III

The lust for revenge – as opposed to the inevitability of retribution – is an emotion almost as ugly as jealousy. Christian forgiveness is a concept alien to those in the grip of either. Fair means or foul will be deployed to settle whatever debts have taken shape in the angry mind; justice, decency and above all reason are lost causes in the whirlwind of emotions propelling the victim to his or her doom. Hamlet is the only character in all Shakespeare to make a point of hesitating over his revenge; it will surely come, sooner or later, but his prolonged delay wrings as much great philosophy from him as it causes him personal grief. There is no moral doubt overshadowing his cause; it is sanctified by his ghostly father himself, who repeatedly returns 'to whet thy almost blunted purpose'. Hamlet has a chance to kill Claudius while he is at prayer; but holds off for the powerful reason that he would be sending the villain to the next world in a state of grace – an option Claudius had not allowed his father, poisoned while sleeping in his orchard. Why, otherwise, does Hamlet delay the full length of a very long five-act play to take his revenge? Four centuries of scholars have failed to resolve this quintessentially Shakespearean question, the whole point of which is that there can be no definitive answer.

Below **Elizabeth Taylor's Katharina is shrewish even towards her sister Bianca.**

APPEARANCE AND REALITY

things are never quite what they seem in Shakespeare's work. The same could be said of his life, which looks like one long attempt to evade detection by posterity. 'He slunk past in life,' as Henry James put it. 'That was good enough for him, the contention appears to be. Why therefore should he not slink past in immortality?' James was eloquently disappointed: 'It is never to be forgotten that we are here in the presence of the human character the most magnificently endowed, in all time… so that of him, inevitably, it goes hardest with us to be told that we have nothing, or next to nothing…'

In fact we have a lot more than Henry James thought, and the most recent discoveries go some way to explaining why Shakespeare seems to have got in the habit of covering his tracks – and thus why he had took such lively interest in his work in disguise, disappearance and dissembling.

Evidence has lately come to light that strongly suggests that the young Shakespeare, brought up an illegal Catholic recusant like his father, was sent straight from school in his mid-teens to the Lancashire household of a titled Catholic family, the de Hoghtons of Hoghton Tower, near Preston, to serve as tutor and part-time actor. In Protestant England, these were dangerous times for Papists; Warwickshire and Lancashire were hotbeds of Catholic recusancy – and the

a midsummer night's dream

spies of Elizabeth's secret service, which was run by the sinister Sir Francis Walsingham, were everywhere. Among those who passed via Warwickshire to Lancashire and Hoghton Tower at this time was the Jesuit priest Edmund Campion, on a secret mission from Rome that saw him eventually arrested and executed – a Catholic martyr, publicly hung, drawn and quartered for his faith.

In Lancashire, at the time of Campion's visit, young Will Shakespeare was known as 'Shakeshaft' – a not uncommon variant of his name, in an age of spell-as-you-please surnames, but also useful as a quasi-alias. Already, it seems, he was trying to give the authorities the slip, to leave no trace of his progress around the country, to adopt guises other than his own. It was a tactic that would stand him in good stead when religion led to ugly, life-and-death politics, as it did in the Gunpowder Plot of 1605 – and which would inform, enliven and further enrich his works.

Shakespeare's plays are full of cross-dressing, disguises, people pretending to be something other than their real selves. His own habit of doing this – offstage, he also had a reputation as a practical joker – has caused four centuries of biographers considerable grief. But, far more importantly, it has also given the glorious canon of his work one of its most characteristic, ingenious and enjoyable dimensions.

'Men should be what they seem,' Iago tells Othello, but of course they never are. In Shakespeare, what you see is rarely what you get. '*Seems*, madam?' Hamlet angrily asks his mother. 'Nay, I know not seems.' Yet the all-too-human Prince of Denmark also spends much of his play pretending to be something other than he is.

So, most obviously, do a wide variety of Shakespeare's leading women, who disguise themselves as young men as they set out on sundry adventures, usually in pursuit of another young man. Which, of course, can lead to complications. It is just as well that the shipwrecked Viola in *Twelfth Night* has an identical twin brother, Sebastian. The Lady Olivia falls in love with the young man sent to woo her by his/her master Orsino, Duke of Illyria; Orsino himself appears to have languid

Nothing is but what is not.

MACBETH, MACBETH, ACT I, SCENE III

longings for him/her; in a complex denouement, the twins believing each other drowned, Olivia can marry Sebastian (believing him to be Viola), the Duke can marry his page by way of compensation; and all, against the odds, can look like living happily ever after.

Similar high jinks enliven the Forest of Arden in *As You Like It*, with Rosalind disguising herself as Ganymede while

pursuing Orlando, exiled son of Sir Roland de Boys. The
pastoral setting (echoing his own mother's family name as
much as a stretch of woodland north of Stratford) was for
Shakespeare as for writers back to the Greek poets and beyond,
a natural, quasi-Utopian setting in which to pit moral values
against each other. Stripped of urban (or so-called 'civilized')
values, the natural world becomes a place where all men are
equal and their self-conduct is seen for what it really is – an
idea eventually explored most fully in *The Tempest*.

All's Well That Ends Well and *Cymbeline* also see young
women disguising themselves as young men, in rather less
happy circumstances, as the only way of pursuing their
romantic goals. It all began in *The Two Gentlemen of Verona*, in
which Shakespeare first reworked an age-old literary device he
was characteristically to make very much his own. Complex
plotting to make the most of cross-dressing in his comedies led

him directly to deeper thinking about the nature of appearances in more sombre settings. *Hamlet* and *Macbeth* are the ultimate in tragic explorations of these themes, where whole worlds are turned upside-down to symbolize the dislocations in nature brought about by men and women pretending to be other than they are – and acting upon their dire self-delusions, invariably with tragic consequences. 'O villain, villain, smiling, damnèd villain,' says Hamlet of his murderous uncle; 'My tables – meet it is I set it down / That one many smile, and smile, and be a villain.'

'Why do you dress me in borrowed robes?' asks Macbeth, launching a play full of clothes imagery, when handed the first of the lofty titles he was planning to pursue by fair means or foul. 'Fair is foul and foul is fair' chant the Three Witches, other-worldly creatures acknowledging the disruption of the natural order in this dark mortal landscape, full of storms, birds

Above **Imogen Stubbs'
cross-dressing Olivia
is confused with her
brother Sebastian in
Trevor Nunn's 1996
Twelfth Night.**

of prey and other ominous portents. Before their crime dooms
them, as if to add to the illusion, the Macbeths are the only
couple in all Shakespeare to have achieved marital harmony.

'Fathers, from hence trust not your daughters' minds /
By what you see them act,' says Desdemona's father, Brabantio,
who (quite rightly, if for the wrong reasons) fears this marriage
will prove disastrous for his daughter. The Moor, of course, is
the ultimate victim of appearances, choosing to turn a blind
eye to reality in an orgy of misguided self-pity. Iago, like
Macbeth's witches, is the only character in the play to see
straight, using his 20/20 vision into other hearts and minds for
his own nefarious purposes. Like the Fool in *Lear*, or the other,
wiser, darker clowns of Shakespeare's later plays, these

apparently peripheral characters are the only ones to keep their priorities straight as whole worlds collapse around them.

So what is Shakespeare saying? That all human beings must strive towards self-knowledge? Nothing quite so simple, as his most villainous characters are often those with the most profound sense of themselves. At the same time, his most virtuous creations can be the most deluded. Anticipating Freud by several centuries, Shakespeare is simply taking a series of large-scale human events, and, without standing in moral judgement, offering the sharpest textbook psychoanalysis of all the leading players. In the opinion of the American scholar Harold Bloom, he was responsible for nothing less than the 'invention' of human personality.

Below **Masked fun-and-games for Emma Thompson and friends in Kenneth Branagh's** *Much Ado About Nothing*.

No wonder Freud wound up among the deluded ranks who waste their breath arguing that Shakespeare didn't write Shakespeare – that a country boy who never went to university was less likely to have written these masterpieces than a better-educated nobleman with a handle to his name: the Earl of Oxford, Sir Francis Bacon, or one of countless other toffs who would never, in truth, have had the time (let alone the talent) to produce so vast and varied a body of work. These are (and always have been) essentially snobbish, class-ridden arguments advanced by people who choose to ignore a raft of documentary evidence that the plays of William Shakespeare were written by the glover's son from Stratford – not even, in a tired old academic joke, by another man of the same name.

Above **Prospero (Heathcote Williams) demonstrates his magic in Derek Jarman's 1979 version of *The Tempest*.**

We are such stuff as dreams are made on…

PROSPERO, THE TEMPEST, ACT IV, SCENE I

So there's no problem with appearance and reality when it comes to the authorship of Shakespeare's work. Yet the poet's obsession with these themes has seen a school of 20th-century scholars reinterpret almost all the plays in these terms – attempting to impose a transient world view on the vast, sprawling canon of his work when, in truth, he is often simply playing elaborate (and fairly arbitrary) games. Part of truth and illusion, after all, is magic and mystery – a world that held an

Far left **The masked Trinculo (Peter Turner) pretends to be a model in Miranda's room in Jarman's adaptation of Shakespeare's last play.**

obvious fascination for Shakespeare from an early play like *A Midsummer Night's Dream* to the fantastical, supernatural goings-on that come to dominate the more benevolent morality of the late romances.

The fairyland in which most of *A Midsummer Night's Dream* takes place, along with the surreal goings-on there – a fairy Queen, for starters, falling in love with an ass – have

*Are you sure
that we are awake? It seems to me
That yet we sleep, we dream.*

DEMETRIUS, A MIDSUMMER NIGHT'S DREAM, ACT IV, SCENE I

between them made the play a Hollywood favourite, from the era of James Cagney and Mickey Rooney to that of Michelle Pfeiffer and Kevin Kline. Just as stage directors and designers hijack this playful text to show off the full extent of their own lurid imaginations, so screen stylists from Max Reinhardt to Peter Hall and Michael Hoffman have taken the chance to make hay with the very latest in special visual effects. Shakespeare would, of course, have been delighted. It is often said that, were he alive today, he would be writing TV soap operas. No, their shallow surface morality would soon have bored him; this poet-playwright would have been far more at home with the subtler avenues open to screenwriters, not to

Above **Designer fairies abound in Adrian Noble's 1996 film of** *A Midsummer Night's Dream.*

mention the vastness of screen audiences, united around the world by the universal language of cinema.

The Tempest, Shakespeare's last solo play, in which he seems to bid a conscious farewell to his art as Prospero breaks his magician's rod and drowns his books, has offered similar enchantments to film-makers – Peter Greenaway and the late Derek Jarman being merely the most recent to recognize the cinematic opportunities available in a magic island immune to the artificially imposed moral code of an external, alien world. 'We are such stuff as dreams are made on' might well (heaven forbid) have been adopted as their motto by studios from Walt Disney to Steven Spielberg, George Lucas and their DreamWorks colleagues.

'... And our little life is rounded with a sleep' – the flip side of Prospero's famous incantation – is Shakespeare's final answer to all the questions imposed by his many and various explorations of truth and illusion, appearance and reality, magic and mystery, morality and retribution. 'What a piece of work is a man?' as Hamlet asks, in the vast universal scheme of things. No more than 'a quintessence of dust.' The universal lessons beneath the grim sequence of events in *Lear*, too, are distilled with similar existential angst by the Earl of Gloucester:

> As flies to wanton boys are we to the gods
>
> They kill us for their sport.

Below Anita Louise's Titania is surrounded by more traditional fairies in Max Reinhardt's 1935 version, with a cast also boasting James Cagney as Bottom and Mickey Rooney as Puck.

Above **Max Reinhardt's stylish visual effects created a truly magical fairyland.**

The mirror that Shakespeare held up to nature was often, quite deliberately, a cracked or distorted one, sometimes the only way to get at the truth by searching for the real reflection. The players he calls 'the abstract and brief chronicles of the time', of whom he himself was proudly one, are of course themselves masters of illusion, purveyors of mere appearances, denizens of disguise. 'The play's the thing' to catch not merely the conscience of a particular, guilty king, but the inner turmoil within all those watching it unfold, seeing reflections of

themselves in the drama enacted before them, measuring its effects upon their own internal demons.

Above **Mickey Rooney's Puck plays tricks on the sleeping Dick Powell's Lysander.**

The theatre, by its very nature, is itself a world of illusion. To Shakespeare, setting up and stripping away layer after layer of wilful fantasy was the most effective way to plumb fundamental truths – about the individual, about society, about the nature of the human condition. Life, after all, is a series of struggles with the forces of delusion. Sometimes the only way to beat them is to play them at their own game.

'g'entle' Will Shakespeare may have been a moderate man in his private habits, but he was never averse to a bit of fun. According to a lawyer-diarist of the day named John Manningham, there was one performance of *Richard III* during which a female fan in the audience approached the playwright's friend Richard Burbage, who was

as you like it playing the title-role, and gamely invited him back to her place after the show. Shakespeare (playing, perhaps, a minor role) must have overheard the furtive conversation in the wings. When Burbage arrived to claim his droit de seigneur, a voice from the lady's chamber told him she wasn't ready for him yet: William the Conqueror had arrived before Richard the Third.

That Shakespeare had a profound, versatile and infinitely subtle sense of humour cannot be in any doubt. He is as capable of creating a gormless clown, muddling his words and falling over his own boots, as he is of crafting the most elegant literary jokes and puns, riddled with allusion to classical literature, for

twelfth night what one of his contemporaries called the 'better sort' of theatregoer. The showman in Shakespeare, as well as the impresario with a stake in the business, was intent on giving as much value for money to the 'groundlings' – the man-off-the-street who had paid a penny to stand through the performance – as to the sixpence-a-seat toff in the upper tiers.

Off-stage, he would play word games in the tavern with Ben Jonson – during one such session they exchanged spoof epitaphs we still possess – and dash off short, jokey poems for friends and acquaintances. On-stage, he could throw a heck of a party – like the Whitsun sheep-shearing celebrations towards the end of *The Winter's Tale*, the longest scene he ever wrote.

But Shakespeare did not share his contemporaries' fondness for the masque, an allegorical revel, usually depicting some formulaic struggle between the forces of virtue and vice, in which the nobility who commissioned the entertainment liked to take part themselves. Ben Jonson wrote countless masques – a playwright was paid as much for a one-act masque as a five act *much ado* tragedy – before even he decided that elaborate designers like Inigo Jones were taking over the show. Even after the accession of King James, who loved performing in masques with his family, Shakespeare preferred to keep the masque firmly in its place, a brief diversion at the end of such plays as *The Tempest*.

Shakespeare was too much of a realist to relish the artifice of the masque. The humour in his plays, high and low, counterpoints their themes, romantic or tragic. The drama does not have to have a happy ending for fun and games to play a central role in the Shakespearean universe.

When Shakespeare first joined the Lord Chamberlain's men, looking after the customers' horses outside the theatre before gradually working his way inside and on-stage, the company's resident comedian was Will Kemp, a legendary vaudeville-style comic beloved of the groundlings. It is because of Kemp that the clowns and other light-relief roles in Shakespeare's early plays indulge in such broad comedy, full of Malapropisms and custard-pie humour. Half-way through his career, when he created the role of the dim-witted Constable Dogberry in *Much Ado About Nothing*, the playwright was thinking of Kemp as much as his own father back in Stratford, who had been the local constable before ascending to the office of Mayor.

After *Much Ado*, however, Shakespeare and Kemp seem to have had some sort of falling-out, as the comedian flounced

We that are true lovers run into strange capers.

TOUCHSTONE, AS YOU LIKE IT, ACT II, SCENE IV

out of the company, rose some money by morris-dancing all the way from London to Norwich, then retired to write a book called *Will Kemp's Nine Days Wonder* in which he attacked his former colleague as 'my notable Shakerags'. Basically, he was complaining that the theatre wasn't what it used to be. Yes, in truth, Kemp seems to have become a bit of a bore. We can hear Shakespeare getting his own back in *Hamlet*, soon after Kemp's

departure, when the theatre-loving Prince of Denmark tells the visiting players:

> Let those that play your clowns speak no more
> than is set down for them; for there be of them
> that will themselves laugh to set on some quantity
> of barren spectators to laugh too, though in the
> mean time some necessary question of the play be
> then to be considered. That's villainous, and shows
> a most pitiful ambition in the fool that uses it.

No ad-libbing, in other words, no laughing at your own jokes, no coming to the front of the stage to milk the audience for laughs. In *Hamlet* Shakespeare rubs home the point by paying fond tribute to the company's original comedian, Richard Tarleton, who is immortalised as Yorick: 'I knew him, Horatio'. Will Kemp, clearly, was no great respecter of the sanctity of Shakespeare's scripts; during some performance of *Much Ado*, perhaps, he ad-libbed once too often; the two men argued and parted company. It was a blessed moment for posterity. Shakespeare's relief is almost audible as Kemp's departure enables him to dispense with low comedy for its own sake. Now he could move on to deeper, darker comic creatures, the Fool in *King Lear* being an interim climax en route to the nihilistic Thersites in *Troilus and Cressida*, the cynical Autolycus in *The Winter's Tale*, the 'noble savage' Caliban in *The Tempest*.

Left Douglas Fairbanks'
1925 Petruchio, despite
his period head-dress,
was equally gung ho.

In Kemp's replacement, Robert Armin, himself also a
writer, Shakespeare was blessed with the perfect vehicle for the
subtler strain of humour inaugurated by Feste in *Twelfth Night*
and Touchstone in *As You Like It*. Like King Lear's Fool, the
exiled Duke Senior's clown is as wise as he is witty, almost to
the point of pedantry. Touchstone has surface wit enough to
keep the groundlings happy, hidden amid classical allusion

Above **Emma Thompson leads some rural frolics in Kenneth Branagh's Tuscan *Much Ado* (1993).**

Previous page **Douglas Fairbanks' Petruchio attempts to find the way to Mary Pickford's heart through her stomach.**

sufficiently erudite to bring a knowing smile to the face of the 'better sort' of theatregoer. While wooing the none-too-bright Audrey, for instance, Touchstone says: 'I am here with thee and thy goats as the most capricious poet honest Ovid was among the Goths.' The melancholy philosopher Jaques, who is eavesdropping, comments: 'O knowledge ill-inhabited, worse than Jove in a thatched house!' Audrey's blank response to such learning would have been echoed by the groundlings, who might enjoy the pun on 'goats' and 'Goths' without sharing the appreciation in the upper tiers of that on 'capricious' (both 'goat-like' and 'horny'), let alone the irony that Ovid – one of Shakespeare's favourite poets since his schooldays – spent his exile among the Goths, or barbarians.

Shakespeare openly acknowledges his relish in this new, more complex vein of humour by having Jaques describe

Touchstone as 'a material fool' – a fool as full of 'wise saws and modern instances' as the gloomy misanthrope himself. The poet also loved theatrical in-jokes, as is clear in the very first line in Jaques' most famous speech, one of the best-known in all Shakespeare, which begins with a hidden translation of the Latin epigram that was the Globe's motto, embroidered on the flag which flew above the stage during performances. *Totus mundus agit histrionem* translates almost literally as 'All the world's a stage' – the opening of Jaques' 'Seven Ages of Man'.

If the humour of an early play like *Love's Labour's Lost* is highly sophisticated, written for private performance before an educated audience in a noble household, Shakespeare's other

Better a witty fool than a foolish wit.

FESTE, TWELFTH NIGHT, ACT I, SCENE V

early comedies are almost farce-like romps. *The Comedy of Errors,* for instance, revolves around an elaborate sequence of mistaken identities as two sets of twins – servants and masters – encounter each other unexpectedly (Rodgers and Hart converted the play into a sprightly 1940 musical, *The Boys from Syracuse*). In *The Taming of the Shrew*, written shortly before *Romeo and Juliet*, the visibly maturing Shakespeare combines slapstick physical comedy with an early exploration of love and marriage, which he continued some five years later in *Much Ado*

Ado About Nothing. The married-divorced-remarried Richard Burton and Elizabeth Taylor, so wonderfully cast in Franco Zeffirelli's lavish 1967 film of *The Shrew*, might well have gone on to play *Much Ado*'s squabbling lovers Benedick and Beatrice as a box-office sequel. By the same token, it is a pity that Kenneth Branagh and his then wife Emma Thompson, equally well-cast in Branagh's elegant 1993 movie of *Much Ado*, never got the chance to give us their Petruchio and Katharina. If the 'golden age' of Hollywood had not been so insistent that Shakespeare was 'box-office poison', Katharine Hepburn and Spencer Tracy would also have been ideal casting as either of these warring couples, whose feelings for each other deepen with every verbal joust.

As Shakespeare embarked on his mightiest works, the great tragedies of the mid-1600s, comedy was put in its place as mere light relief from dark and diabolical deeds; the Porter in *Macbeth*, for instance, with his complex quips about Catholic 'equivocators', and his groundling jokes about drink and sex, builds the suspense between the murder of Duncan and the discovery of his body. In *King Lear*, by contrast, the Fool plays a central role in the unfolding drama, licensed to tell the misguided monarch home truths no other courtier could get away with; it is through the wisdom behind his impertinent remarks that Lear begins to rediscover himself (whom he has known 'ever but slenderly').

In the late plays, exemplified by *The Winter's Tale*, comedy symbolizes the redemption the mature playwright allows his tragic heroes and heroines. After three acts of the grimmest tragedy, in which Leontes' unfounded doubts about his wife's fidelity appears to cost him her and both their children, the king finds his tortured way back to her amid the permanent party that is pastoral Bohemia. Autolycus is the last of Shakespeare's clowns, and one of the most boldly written; this 'snapper-up of unconsidered trifles' is part-unscrupulous con man, part-loveable rogue, around whom the carnival chaos of the last two acts coheres.

Only ten of Shakespeare's 38 plays can truly be called comedies, but fun and games play a vital role in almost all, if

Below 'Fulvia perchance is angry' (Cleopatra, *Antony and Cleopatra*, act I, scene i). Hildegard Neil's Cleopatra taunts Charlton Heston's Antony over his wife's jealousy (1973).

Left Oberon gives Puck his orders in Celestino Coronada's Anglo-Spanish *A Midsummer Night's Dream* (1984).

only to relieve bleaker pressures. He may have preferred dark, searching comedy, as in *All's Well That Ends Well*, but he also knew that slapstick put bums on seats. As did Queen Elizabeth, who so much enjoyed the character of Falstaff in *Henry IV* that she demanded a play showing 'Sir John in love'. The result was *The Merry Wives of Windsor*, knocked off in a couple of weeks to gratify the monarch's whim. And it shows. That he did not put too much effort into his least funny comedy suggests that Shakespeare was none too pleased to be diverted from his work on his second historical tetralogy.

Below Director's imaginations often run riot in *A Midsummer Night's Dream*, as in Celestino Coronada's 1984 version, where Titania is one among many fairyland grotesques.

Throughout the canon, Shakespeare rarely savoured as much magical, fantastical fun and games as in *A Midsummer Night's Dream* – another exploration of marriage, at heart, in which several more warring couples are played off against each other. Oberon and Titania, king and queen of the fairies, are really 'shadows' of Duke Theseus and his wife Hipployta, who learn much about their own marriage from the antics of their imaginary equivalents. The punishment Oberon inflicts on

My Oberon! What visions have I seen!
I thought I was enamoured of an ass!

TITANIA, A MIDSUMMER NIGHT'S DREAM, ACT IV, SCENE I

Titania, casting a spell which sees her fall in love with an ass, inevitably rebounds on him, teaching all lovers throughout the ages the lessons of give and-take. In Bottom the Weaver, who doubles as the tragicomic ass, Shakespeare created an off-the-wall character who has as much fun as any in the entire canon.

And this convoluted plot was one of only three in 38 – the other two being *Love's Labour's Lost* and *The Tempest* – that Shakespeare plucked from his own imagination, rather than some pre-existing primary source.

Just as we cannot permit ourselves to call comedy Shakespeare's natural habitat, so we cannot deny that it was a genre in which he felt very much at home.

POWER AND POLITICS

*S*hakespeare does not seem to have been a particularly political animal. Which is to say: he was suspicious of supreme rulers, while seeing deep into their motives, vulnerabilities and aspirations; distrusted courtiers, relishing every chance to puncture their pomposity; and sided instinctively with the common man, this side of handing him the reins of *richard II* power. He understood, and was fascinated by, politics and politicians; but, despite a front-row seat, took little if any active part in the turbulent events of his age.

Towards the end of Elizabeth I's long reign Shakespeare's patron, the Earl of Southampton, and his mentor, the Earl of Essex, were both jailed (and Essex eventually beheaded) for their political and religious convictions. Shakespeare seemed content to watch from a safe distance – sympathizing, no doubt, not least as a fellow Catholic, but reluctant to play any active role. As one of the King's Men, when James VI of Scotland succeeded the Virgin Queen as James I of England, Shakespeare even became a member of the royal *julius caesar* household, issued with scarlet cloth for his livery. But, again, he seems content to have lurked in the wings, doing whatever was necessary to maintain a writer's quiet life: trying to retain the king's favour without joining the sycophants, choosing themes for plays to gratify the monarch's intellectual interests without stooping to hagiography.

The instinctive sympathy of the Stratford poet, self-made son of a self-made businessman, was clearly with the people rather than their rulers. Not until Lear is naked on the heath, deprived of his royal support-system and forced to realize that even a king is just another 'poor, bare, fork'd animal' like any other mere mortal, does he begin to approach self-knowledge. But it is hard not to feel that in certain moods Shakespeare shares some of the contempt for the mob, fickle as it can be, with which he fills the warrior-turned-politician Coriolanus.

Shakespeare took political risks in his work, reinterpreting comparatively recent events in his history plays, and slyly reflecting controversial current affairs in many others. But he was as interested in the general as in the particular, in the fundamental lessons to be learned about human nature – and

coriolanus morals to be drawn about man's inhumanity to man – than in ephemeral satire. That is why so many of his plays still carry such resonance for our own times, as they have for every era since his own. Shakespeare's unique insights into man's mind and character echo Machiavelli as much as anticipating Freud. What is a politician, after all, what is a king or queen or courtier but another human being quite as fallible as those over whom he or she seeks to exercise control? This is the central moral of Shakespeare's political work, just as it is the daily agenda of our newspapers and TV news bulletins to this day.

On 6 February 1601 some aristocratic followers of the Earl of Essex came to the Globe with a request that the Lord Chamberlain's men mount a performance of Shakespeare's *Richard II* – complete with its controversial 'deposition scene', in which Henry Bolingbroke usurps the place of the rightful, divinely anointed ruler. In vain did the company protest that

Right In his own 1996 film, Kenneth Branagh's Hamlet was 'likely, had he been put on, / To have prov'd most royal' (Fortinbras, *Hamlet*, act V, scene ii).

the play was past its prime, that it would scarcely fill the theatre. With Essex poised to attempt a coup against the ageing Queen, the actors must have realized the political significance, and thus the potential dangers, of what they were being asked to do. But the conspirators offered to underwrite the performance, to the tune of 40 shillings beyond the

Above **In Roman
Polanski's 1971 film,
Martin Shaw's Banquo
puzzles over the
Witches' prophecies with
Jon Finch's Macbeth.**

standard fee and box-office percentage. How could mere
players refuse such a lucrative commission from insistent
eminences of high birth?

Unlike Essex, the actors got away with it – just. The sworn
deposition of Shakespeare's colleague and friend Augustine
Phillips persuaded the ferocious investigator, Francis Bacon,
that their involvement was purely theatrical. But it was an
object lesson for Shakespeare in how dangerously close to
home day-to-day politics could intrude.

Five years later he took a calculated risk in presenting his
new Scottish monarch and patron with a play about the

assassination of a Scottish king. The previous year, 1605, had seen an attempt on James' life by Catholic dissidents in the notorious 'Powder Treason', today better-known as the Gunpowder Plot, in which Robert Catesby, Guy Fawkes and

Uneasy lies the head that wears a crown.

KING HENRY, HENRY IV PART 2, ACT III, SCENE I

others tried to blow up the monarch and his peers (including many fellow Catholics) at the Opening of Parliament. Boldly, Shakespeare filled *Macbeth* with references to Catholic oppression and restive political dissidents. Guilefully, meanwhile, he flattered the king's interest in witchcraft, on which he had recently published a treatise, by diverting him with the three Weird Sisters.

Macbeth was riddled with references to the Powder Treason, only too clear to contemporary audiences. Its running theme of 'equivocation' made topical play of the Jesuit doctrine by which a prisoner under interrogation might in good conscience disguise the truth to avoid incriminating himself. In the Porter's speech Shakespeare was making light of a serious matter once close to his recusant heart. Elsewhere in the play, he pays his most serious attention (as would James and his government) to the prevailing moral belief that equivocation was a surrender to the forces of evil, tantamount

Far right, top 'Friends, Romans, countrymen, lend me your ears' (Marc Antony, *Julius Caesar*, act III, scene ii). Marlon Brando delivers Marc Antony's famous funeral oration for Julius Caesar (1953).

to an alliance with the devil. The Weird Sisters are temptresses dragging Macbeth, via his own equivocations, into just such a Faustian pact. But Shakespeare stresses that he makes it of his own free will – riddled with eloquent, equivocal doubts that render him, both before and after his crime, an unlikely Everyman who can resist everything except temptation.

Does Macbeth really see the witches, the dagger, Banquo's ghost? Of course he does, even if others don't. James certainly believed so; as James VI of Scotland, the son of an assassin's victim, he had been deeply disturbed by the discovery of a waxen image of himself, made with murderous intent by his mother's third husband, the Earl of Bothwell. So the King would have savoured Macbeth's entanglement with the Weird Sisters. Such figures, to him, were no mere fantasies; they represented, as in Shakespeare's play, a central facet of man's continuing earthly struggle against the ubiquitous powers of evil.

Whatever his private feelings (which leave room for doubt), James also affected to believe in the ancient tradition, dating back to Edward the Confessor, of the power of the 'King's touch' to cure scrofula and other diseases. It handily buttressed another aspect of monarchy he was at pains to reassert – the 'Divine Right' of kings, chosen and anointed by God, thus rendering any attempt on their lives blasphemy as well as treason. For all his distaste at mingling with *hoi polloi*, let alone touching their running sores, James had recently

Far right, bottom Brando's Marc Antony remonstrates with Caesar's murderers.

revived the practice of 'touching' the afflicted, earning himself another courtly nod from Shakespeare via an eyewitness account from Duncan's son and heir, Malcolm, exiled at the London court. Shakespeare paid further tribute to James' ancestry in the Parade of Kings at the end of the play – while offering his royal patron the supreme compliment of keeping *Macbeth* so short that critics have worried that some of the text might be lost. Shakespeare, in his way, was a smart politician: he knew that James was prone to fall asleep if a play lasted more than two hours.

Far left **Hildegard Neil's Cleopatra was every inch a Queen.**

> *The abuse of greatness is when it disjoins*
> *Remorse from power...*
>
> BRUTUS, JULIUS CAESAR, ACT II, SCENE I

Between the lines, of course, the playwright is also offering his monarch somewhat risqué advice. Power, he is constantly saying, corrupts. Richard III and Macbeth are obvious examples of rulers corrupted as much by the quest for power as the exercise of it (the historical Macbeth, in fact, was a successful and popular ruler for ten years). Lear (like James) carries all the faults of too many hereditary monarchs: vain, self-obsessed, insistent on absurd privilege, heedless of the everyday woes of his subjects. Julius Caesar is clearly an excellent ruler; but power has gone to his head, and it is

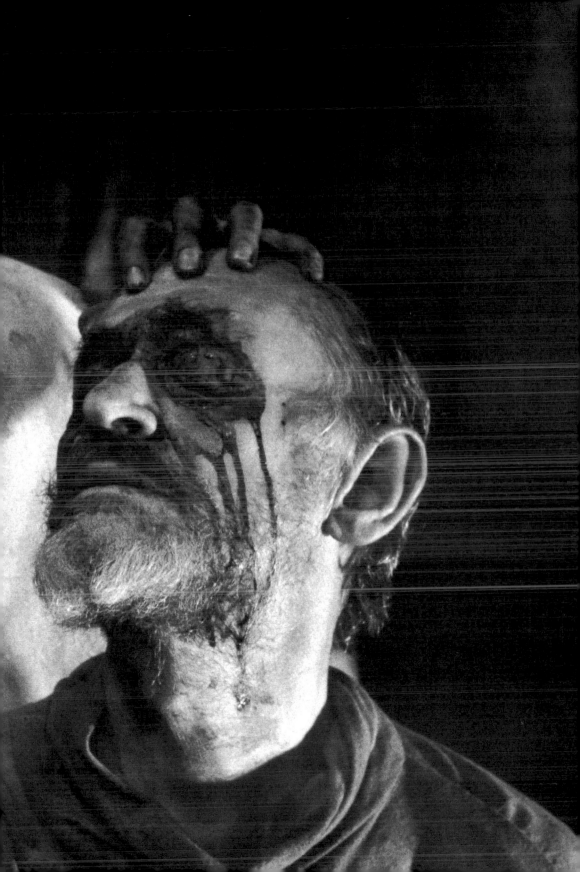

with feigned reluctance that he turns aside the crown. Among all Shakespeare's monarchs, perhaps only Henry V has his priorities right: seeking his nation's welfare before his own. He may have been a much more appealing figure as the high-spirited young Prince Hal, wassailing with his friend Falstaff; but his rejection of Falstaff ('I know thee not, old man'), in one of Shakespeare's most affecting scenes, is a necessary part of his transition to the throne.

In Antony and Cleopatra we see a rare example of two mighty rulers and noble spirits who, after a lifetime of the enlightened exercise of power, throw the world away for love. In Lear we see a king who throws his kingdom away for vanity – which also dooms Julius Caesar. In *Measure for Measure*, inspired by James' inconsistent dispensation of justice during his journey south to assume the English throne, we see a weak

Above and far left
'Once more unto the breach, dear friends' (Henry, *King Henry V*, act III, scene i). Laurence Olivier's 1944 *Henry V* (above) and Kenneth Branagh's 1989 version (far left).

> We have kissed away
> Kingdoms and provinces.

SCARUS, ANTONY AND CLEOPATRA, ACT III, SCENE X

ruler hand his power to a more powerful surrogate who is immediately corrupted by it. Even when Shakespeare's intent is to discuss quite other human failings, such as jealousy, envy, ingratitude (as in *Timon of Athens*), he does so via those of rulers, politicians, people of power.

Previous page Susan Engel's callous Regan exults over the blinded Gloucester (Alan Webb) in Peter Brook's 1971 film of *King Lear*.

Such a philosopher is Hamlet, such an exemplar of idealistic, introspective, prematurely world-weary youth, that we often forget he is also a political animal as much as a military man. Denmark's was an elective monarchy, but Hamlet felt he was entitled to a good chance of succeeding his father on the throne. Polonius, a quasi-Prime Minister who has loyally helped steer the country through turbulent times, is

Right Branagh's
Henry V rides into the
Battle of Agincourt.

no fool; but Hamlet is perpetually intent on making him appear so, for reasons beyond his semblance of madness.

The fatalism of *Hamlet*, so appealing to the existential angst of four centuries of adolescents, curdled to the bleak nihilism of *Troilus and Cressida*, the darkest, most pessimistic play Shakespeare ever wrote. He took the ancient legend of the war-separated lovers, which he had known in Chaucer's version since his schooldays, and turned it into more than a mere indictment of inconstancy, or just another fable of man's inhumanity to man. In this work more than any other, a broad

Above Olivier's Henry V marries Katherine of France (Renée Asherson).

array of characters – most of them worldly leaders – fail to live up to their own ideals. They are all talk and no action, until eventually goaded by the basest of motives, a far remove from the ideals they claim to represent. Few have many redeeming features. The only character in the entire play who remains true to himself throughout, and consistently speaks the most sense, is the cynical, vagabond clown Thersites – the forerunner of a series of increasingly dark fools and clowns, invariably wiser than their masters. Of all Shakespeare's plays, *Troilus and Cressida* has been uniquely adopted by the 20th century, apparently the first since his own day to find sombre echoes of itself in his cerebral vision of a world collapsed by war.

In these great tragedies, as throughout his history plays, Shakespeare is as much as political commentator as a poetic seer of the human soul. Human nature is such that his kings are always looking over their shoulders – quite rightly – for potential assassins, people after their jobs. But those in office, however they got there, are forever prone to the corruptions of office. Retaining power becomes as much of a priority as exercising it; and that exercise is all too often self-interested, with personal security a higher priority than the general good. Shakespeare's portrayals of those in high office anticipate a prevailing contemporary cynicism: it is a rare Shakespearean politician who seeks or exercises power for the benefit of anyone but his or her self.

Far left, top 'I am not in the giving vein today' (Richard, *Richard III*, act IV, scene ii). After his coronation, Olivier's Richard betrays Ralph Richardson's Buckingham.

Far left, bottom Ian McKellen's Richard III (1995) scowls from his bloodily-won throne.

by all accounts, Shakespeare was a good-willed, genial, gentle soul, perhaps even rather shy, who rarely crossed the wrong person, made few enemies, was universally liked and admired. A man of moderation in all things, according to the diarist John Aubrey, he would usually invent an excuse – tell a white lie, pretend that he had a headache – if invited by his

richard III

theatrical pals to go on a 'debauch', the Elizabethan equivalent of a pub-crawl. He may not have been much of a father to his growing children, absent throughout most of their young lives, but he was described by all who knew him as the warmest, most loyal and trustworthy of friends.

And yet this apparent paragon of virtue managed to create some of the most evil characters who ever trod a stage (or a page) and lingered on to haunt all our dreams, perhaps our nightmares. From the brutish Aaron in one of his earliest plays, *Titus Andronicus*, to *Richard III*, Iago in *Othello*, Iachimo in *Cymbeline* and many, many more, Shakespeare plucked from his fertile imagination men and women

king lear

to make your flesh creep, to fill you with doubts about the delicate balance of human nature, to help you peer over otherwise unvisited cliffs of character at the darker slopes of humankind.

At the same time, he was blessed with a matchless ability to create those characters who normally defeat the greatest of writers: the noble, the virtuous, the uncomplicatedly good. These kinds of people may be less fun from the writer's point of view, and occasionally the reader's or audience's, but they are far harder to depict convincingly. And few of Shakespeare's decent, good-hearted characters – Horatio in *Hamlet* or Kent, Gloucester and Edgar in *King Lear* – ever bore or irritate us. *othello* The too-good-to-be-true are rare indeed, though some may think this of such inflexibly righteous figures as the priggish Isabella in *Measure for Measure*.

'Goodness', to Shakespeare, was not an especially religious concept, any more than the evil that lurks within all men. Though raised a Roman Catholic, his own faith seems to have deserted him, and he apparently ended his days a somewhat nihilistic humanist. Given the strict laws of the day, and the highly-charged religious atmosphere, his work was obliged to observe certain orthodoxies and conventions, or it would have been ordered off the stage by Her Majesty's Master of the Revels, Sir Edmund Tilney. But Shakespeare's depictions of good and evil transcend merely religious niceties; they transform the normal Christian world-view that informs most decent lives into a less formulaic look at the world as it really is, a world in which evil can triumph over virtue lived in vain, a world haunted as much by the forces of the devil as by any god, but in which the wicked cannot avoid their comeuppance, and moral decency will eventually – however long it takes – prevail.

Right Alan Bates'
corrupt Claudius broods
about the dangers posed
by Hamlet, the son whom
Glenn Close's innocent
Gertrude so loves.

In 1608, after the mighty creative burst of the great tragedies
and the late Roman plays, Shakespeare and his colleagues in
the King's Men took over a second theatre to counterpoint the
Globe: a smaller, indoor theatre across the river called the
Blackfriars. In an auditorium with a roof, lit only by tapers, the
playwright could embark on yet another, completely different
phase of work – the last one, as it transpired, comprising the
late plays from *Pericles* and *Cymbeline* to *The Winter's Tale* and
The Tempest. The plays he wrote for the winter season at the

*There is nothing either good or bad but thinking
makes it so...*

HAMLET, HAMLET, ACT II, SCENE II

Blackfriars would, of course, transfer to the Globe in summer
– twice as many paying customers swelling his already
handsome annual income – but now he could write far more
intimate scenes than the outdoor, 2,000-seat Globe had let
him dare. One of the first examples of this 'new' late
Shakespeare, in the second act of *Cymbeline*, constitutes one of
the most thrillingly evil stage-pictures he ever painted.

The villainous Iachimo tiptoes around the sleeping (and
thus so vulnerable) Imogen's chamber, where he has been
hiding in a trunk while she went to bed. By the light of a single
torch, he notes down the room's contents: the paintings, the

Previous page

In Hamlet's wild and whirling world, he must shoulder the blame for the tragic descent of Ophelia (Helena Bonham Carter) into madness and eventual suicide (Zeffirelli, 1990).

window, the bedclothes, the pictures on the arras. Then he leans over the sleeping girl herself, notes the title of the volume of Ovid left open on her bedside table, removes her bracelet, inspects the mole on her left breast, is even tempted to kiss her. 'How bravely thou becom'st thy bed!' the dastardly knave whispers over the sleeping beauty.

> Fresh lily,
> And whiter than the sheets! That I might touch,
> But kiss, one kiss!… 'Tis her breathing that
> Perfumes the chamber thus. The flame o' th' taper
> Bows toward her, and would underpeep her lids,
> To see th' enclosèd lights, now canopied
> Under these windows, white and azure-laced
> With blue of heaven's own tinct.

The terrifying beauty of this scene had the doctor-diarist Simon Forman holding his breath when he saw *Cymbeline* in April 1611. 'Remember,' he recorded in his notebook, 'in the deepest of that night, she being asleep, he opened the chest and came forth of it, and viewed her in her bed, and the marks of her body; and took away her bracelet…' The scene would be almost as effective, of course, during the play's seasonal transfer to the Globe; before the Blackfriars, however, Shakespeare might not have been minded to write it.

Far right **Jean Simmons' pre-Raphaelite Ophelia drowns herself in Olivier's 1948 *Hamlet*.**

Before the Blackfriars, his portraits of evil were swaggering monsters like the crookback Richard III, who takes such

engaging relish in his own iniquities; Macbeth, wracked by
guilt over his; and above all Iago, who shares Richard's
self-satisfaction in his own satanic skills. The poison Iago
pours in Othello's ear begins almost imperceptibly, when he
mutters 'I like not that' as across the stage Cassio takes his
innocent leave of Desdemona. 'What dost thou say?' asks
Othello, falling right into his ensign's wily trap. 'Nothing, my
lord,' replies Iago, 'or if – I know not what.'

But Othello's curiosity has been ingeniously aroused. 'Was
not that Cassio parted from my wife?' he asks, and Iago drives

home his first poisoned dart:

> Cassio, my lord? No, sure, I cannot think it,
>
> That he would steal away so guilty-like,
>
> Seeing your coming.

Othello is doomed from that moment. As he swiftly takes Iago's bait, Desdemona plays her unwitting role in both their downfalls by coming over to plead repeatedly for her husband's

I hate the Moor; my cause is hearted…

IAGO, OTHELLO, ACT I, SCENE III

pardon for his lieutenant Cassio, framed by Iago in a drunken brawl the night before. Again, we can but marvel at Iago's clinical fiendishness, and weep at the mighty Othello's gullibility. No matter how often you see or read it, this is drama to stiffen the hairs on the back of your neck, to have any audience transfixed with powerless horror and dismay.

'Demand me nothing,' says Iago at the last, when his machinations have duly seen his master murder his innocent young wife. 'What you know, you know. / From this time forth I never shall speak word.' Foiled by his own wife's horrified honesty, Iago shows no trace of guilt as he is led away to face his just deserts. This is Shakespeare at his most blood-curdling; the villainous bastard Don John in *Much Ado* is, similarly, 'not a man of many words'. Even Richard of

Above 'Give me the daggers!' (Lady Macbeth, *Macbeth*, act II, scene ii). Judith Anderson's Lady Macbeth (1960) proves as murderous as her husband.

Far right 'Is this a dagger which I see before me' (Macbeth, *Macbeth*, act II, scene i). Jon Finch's Macbeth contemplates the murder of Duncan.

Gloucester (the creation of a much younger Shakespeare) is contrite, in his own bleak way, as he faces defeat and death:

My conscience hath a thousand several tongues,

And every tongue brings in a several tale,

And every tale condemns me for a villain.

Like Macbeth, Richard is haunted by the ghosts of his victims. But Macbeth is a less willing accomplice of the devil (in the human form of the three Witches); as his terrifying wife meditates, he is 'too full of the milk of human kindness to catch the nearest way'.

'We will proceed no further in this business,' her husband soon tires to tell her. Macbeth has changed his mind about killing Duncan; their potential victim is his kinsman, his king, his benefactor; why, he might even become king himself without resorting to regicide, 'the deep damnation of his taking off.' But Lady Macbeth, the most malignant woman in all Shakespeare, has got the bit between her teeth. She, too, wants the crown, and she doesn't care how she gets it. Not for her Macbeth's doubts and hesitations. 'Unsex me here,' she prays to her own deities, 'And fill me from the crown to toe full of the direst cruelty...

Come to my woman's breasts

And take my milk for gall, you murdering ministers,

Wherever in your sightless substances,

You wait on nature's mischief.

As their undeserving victim, Duncan is portrayed as a paragon among monarchs, who 'hath borne his faculties so meek, hath been / So clear in his great office, that his virtues / Will plead like angels, trumpet-tongu'd' against his murder. 'This castle hath a pleasant seat,' declares the king, with heavy irony to our ears, as he arrives as the Macbeths' house-guest for what will prove his last night on earth.

Shakespeare's portraits of evil must naturally be juxtaposed with those of goodness; like Duncan, Desdemona is fleshed out far less than those around her, so as to remain unsullied in our eyes, an affecting victim less for who she is than for the rank unfairness of what happens to her. In *King Lear*, likewise, Edgar's pristine virtue counterpoints his bastard brother Edmund's villainy, to the point of stretching our credulity, while Kent and Gloucester soldier loyally on through countless

I grow, I prosper;
Now, gods, stand up for bastards!

EDMUND, KING LEAR, ACT I, SCENE II

insults and humiliations. All in vain; Lear finally regains his senses, but his cause is lost. This is Shakespeare at his bleakest, three-quarters of the way through his writing career. Just before he offers his audiences some hope of redemption, in the late plays, he treats them almost sadistically. But, in the totality

of the canon as in most of the plays, virtue in the shape of simple human decency eventually prevails.

Hamlet, as so often, offers the supreme example. Claudius lives long enough to enjoy the fruits of his appalling crime: the murder of his brother. He savours the throne, the love of his victim's wife, the slavish loyalty of his turncoat courtiers in pursuing his dangerous nephew's life. Justice may finally be done, but Claudius has a good run for his money. He would probably, given the chance, take nothing back.

'Some rise by sin, and some by virtue fall,' Shakespeare had observed in *Measure for Measure*, elegantly summing up the fulcrum of so much of his work for the stage. The Stratford

Above 'Was ever woman in this humour won?' (Richard, *Richard III*, act I, scene ii). Laurence Olivier's Richard III woos Claire Bloom's Lady Anne (1955).

Far right 'Now is the winter of our discontent…' (Richard, *Richard III*, act I, scene i). No actor has ever delivered Richard III's famous opening speech as lethally as Olivier.

man did not always observe the moralistic Hollywood code, developed (if unwittingly) from ancient Greek tragedy, that wrongdoing must always be swiftly punished. The forces of evil often get their wicked way in Shakespeare, and enjoy the fruits of their misbegotten labours for some time before retribution duly catches up with them. Shakespeare, like life, is never black-and-white; it is in the shades of grey, expressed in the most powerful dramatic poetry ever written, that his true greatness – and his appeal to generations beyond his own, past, present and future – finally lies.

Love and hate; death and retribution; jealousy and revenge; appearance and reality; fun and games; power and politics; good and evil: these central themes in Shakespeare's work have offered but one way to look at his remarkable universality, which ultimately evades whatever pigeon-holes each age tries to force upon it. In his work as in his life, Shakespeare evades mere categorization, and rises above analysis. He avoids detection, slipping away to watch from the wings as we marvel at his power to hold his mirror up to our nature, to tell us the most profound truths about ourselves, whatever age we live in. So it is that each succeeding generation sees itself reflected in Shakespeare's timeless wisdom, its own joys and pains, triumphs and tragedies acted out on his eternal stage. To paraphrase Shakespeare himself: age cannot wither, nor custom stale his infinite variety.

Far left **Ian McKellen's Richard III (1995)** was a mid-20th century neo-Nazi.

INDEX

Illustrations from films are denoted by year, director(s) of film, followed by page references in *italic*. The caption to the illustration may not be on the same page as the illustration itself. Characters in the plays are indexed from text only.

ACKNOWLEDGEMENTS

Picture acknowledgements are given in source order

Mary Evans Picture Library Endpapers.

The Ronald Grant Archive Cannon Italia *150*; Castle Rock Entertainment *16–17*, *21* bottom, *40* bottom right, *120–121*, *146* top; Cabochon Productions *114*; Channel Four *112–113*; Columbia Pictures *24*; Cressida Film Productions *72–73*; Dino De Laurentis 69 top; Grand Prize Productions 82; ICON front cover bottom centre left, bottom right, back cover bottom centre left, *2*, *21* top, *22–23*, *42–43*, *60–61*, *140*, *142–143*; London Film Productions 51 top, 134 top, 152 top, 153; Mercury Productions 71 top right; MGM 125 bottom; Playboy Productions *122* top; Renaissance Films *35* top, *70* top, *108* top, *130*, *136–137*; Royal Film Productions *31* top right, *32* top, *75* bottom; RSC *91* top; Transac *50*; Twentienth Century Fox front cover centre left, *44* bottom, *56–57*, *69* bottom; Two Cities *131* top right, *145*.

Kobal Collection BBC/NT *83* top; BHE/Warner Bros *34*; Boyd's Company *86*, *87* top right; Caliban/Playboy/Columbia *46*, *149*; Cannon Films *49* bottom; Capital/Edenwood/Arts Council *92* top right; Columbia Pictures *101*, *102–103*; Electrovision/Warner Bros 67 top; Elton/Pickford/United Artists *33*, *105*, *106–107*; Filmways/Laterna/Athena/RSC *128–129*; Grand Prize/British Lion/Davis Boulton *148* top left; Hepworth *81* top; MGM *29*; Paramount/ABHE *30*; Rank/Folio Films *111* bottom, *126*; Renaissance Films back cover bottom right, *116–117*; Sovexport *54* bottom; Two Cities/Pilgrim/Rank/Wilfrid Newton *20* top left, *40* top left, *64–65*, *133* top; Warner Bros *88–89*, *93* bottom, *94* top, *95* top.

The Moviestore Collection Commonwealth United Entertainment (UK) Ltd *52–53*; Mercury/Republic back cover centre right, *14*; MGM *125* top; Miramax *8–9*, *11*; Paramount Pictures back cover bottom left, *36–37*; Renaissance Films Plc *41* top, *84* top, *85* bottom, *96–97*, *132* bottom left; Turner Pictures/Castle Rock Entertainment/Columbia Pictures Corporation *62–63*; Twentieth Century Fox front cover bottom left, *27* top, *76–77*, *91* bottom; United Artists *134* bottom, *154*; Universal International front cover bottom centre right, *41*.

How many ag[es]

Shall this

...es unborn and